6 7 8 9 10 6 7

Jenny Ackland

Fun with
Counting

OXFORD
UNIVERSITY PRESS

6 7 8 9 10 6 7

Introduction

These workbooks introduce and reinforce basic numeracy and literacy concepts for pre-school and Reception Year children. They give children opportunities to develop and practise some of the skills that are assessed in the Foundation Stage Profile, which is completed before the children move up into Year 1. The activities should be fun and are designed to stimulate discussion as well as practical skills. Some children will be able to complete activities alone, after initial discussion; others may benefit from adult support throughout.

Fun with Counting offers a variety of activities which focus, in particular, on the following:

- revision of numbers 1 to 5

- counting and recognizing numbers 0 to 10

- sequencing numbers up to 10

- understanding 'more' and 'less'

- basic addition and subtraction

- recognition of numbers 1 to 20 (where appropriate).

Oxford University Press
Great Clarendon Street, Oxford OX2 6DP

Oxford University Press is a department of the University of Oxford.
It furthers the University's objective of excellence in research, scholarship, and education by publishing worldwide in
Oxford New York Auckland Cape Town Dar es Salaam Hong Kong Karachi
Kuala Lumpur Madrid Melbourne Mexico City Nairobi New Delhi
Shanghai Taipei Toronto

With offices in
Argentina Austria Brazil Chile Czech Republic France Greece Guatemala
Hungary Italy Japan Poland Portugal Singapore South Korea Switzerland
Thailand Turkey Ukraine Vietnam

Oxford is a registered trade mark of ©Oxford University Press
in the UK and in certain other countries

© Jenny Ackland 2005
The moral rights of the author have been asserted
Database right Oxford University Press (maker)
First published 2005

British Library Cataloguing in Publication Data
Data available

ISBN-10: 0-19-838432-7
ISBN-13: 978-0-19-838432-8
Pack of 6
ISBN-10: 0-19-838430-0
ISBN-13: 978-0-19-838430-4
Pack of 36
ISBN-10: 0-19-838431-9
ISBN-13: 978-0-19-838431-1

1 3 5 7 9 10 8 6 4 2

Designed by Red Face Design
Illustrations by Mark Brierley, Sue Cony
Printed in China

Contents

Numbers 1 to 5

Write the numbers and count the animals.

1 | | | |

2 2 2 2 2

3 3 3 3 3

4 4 4 4 4

5 5 5 5 5

Sets of 5

Circle and colour the sets of 5.

Missing numbers

Fill in the missing numbers.

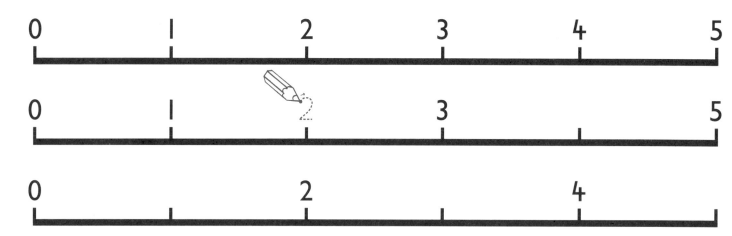

Read the numbers and draw the spots.

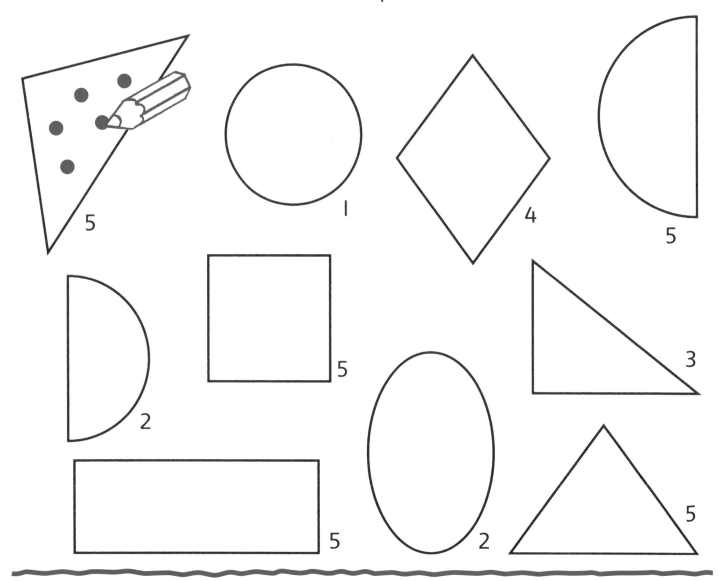

Recognizing sets

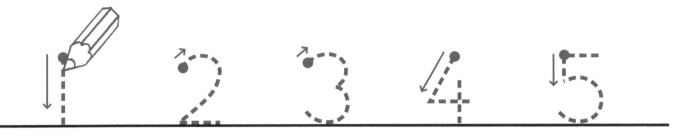

Read each sentence and fill in the missing number.

There are _____ cars.   There are _____ birds.

There are _____ dogs.   There are _____ trees.

Number 6

Circle and colour the sets of 6.

Counting 6

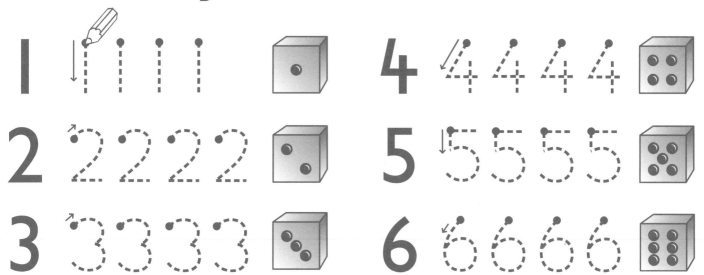

Give each cat 6 whiskers.

Number 7

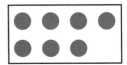

Circle and colour the sets of 7.

Counting 7

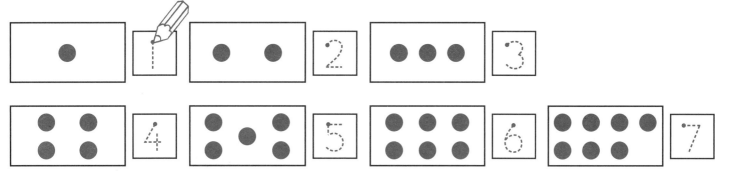

Draw and colour 7 balloons.

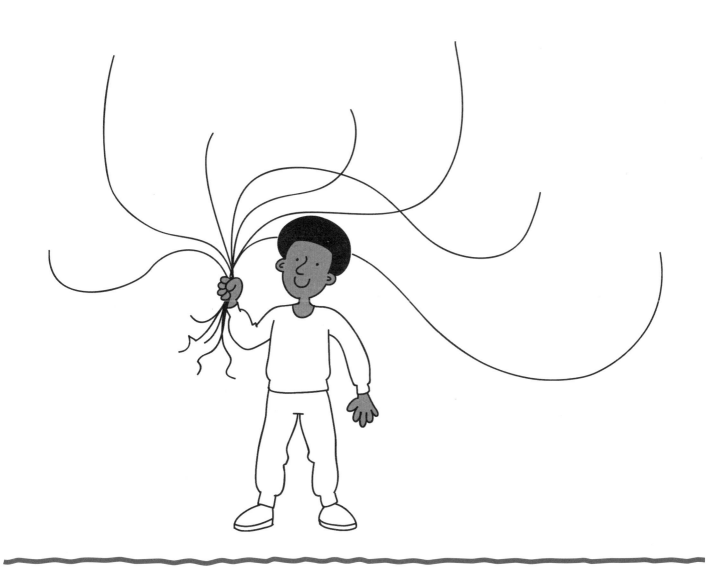

Sets of 7

Circle and colour the sets of 7.

Counting to 7

How many birds are there? Circle the right number.

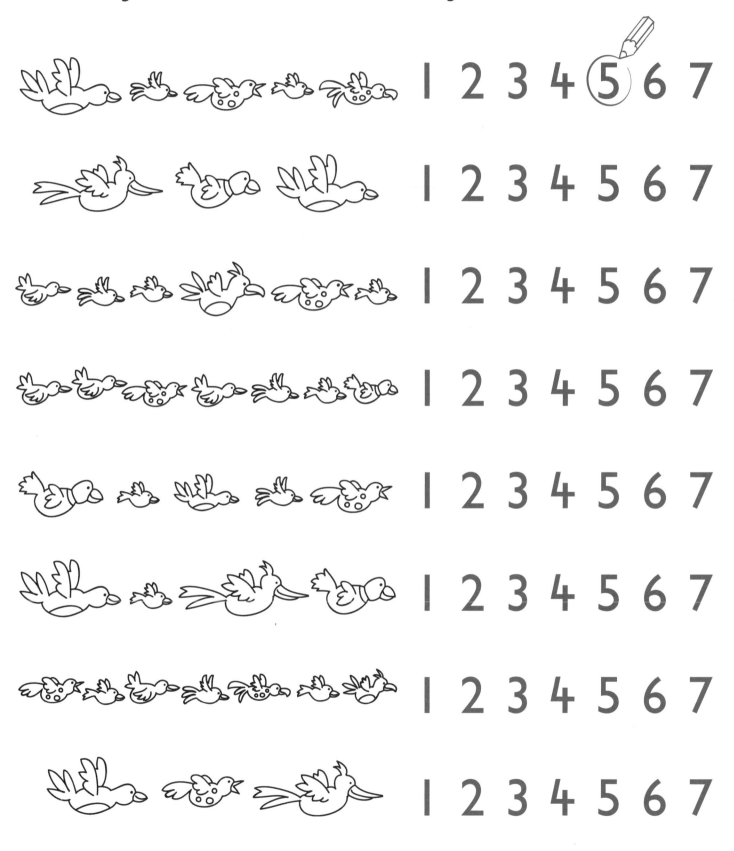

1 2 3 4 (5) 6 7

1 2 3 4 5 6 7

1 2 3 4 5 6 7

1 2 3 4 5 6 7

1 2 3 4 5 6 7

1 2 3 4 5 6 7

1 2 3 4 5 6 7

1 2 3 4 5 6 7

Number 8

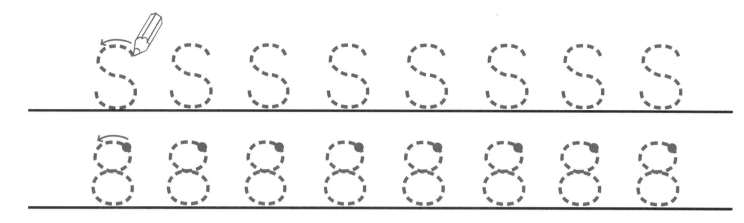

Give this bug 8 legs. Colour them.

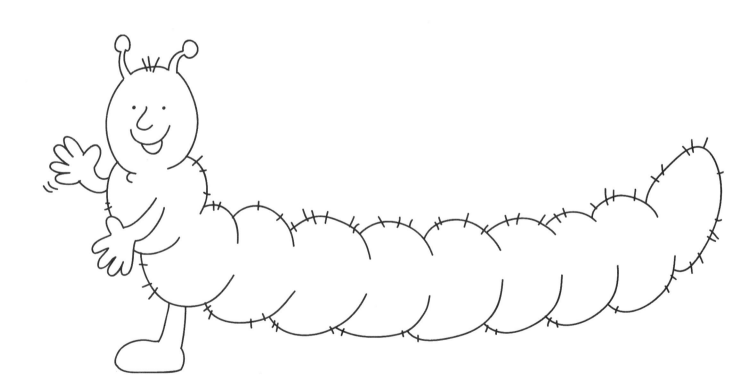

Counting to 8

Draw the dots on these dominoes.

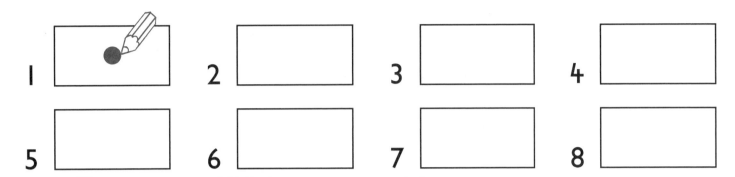

1   2   3   4

5   6   7   8

Count the people and circle the right number.

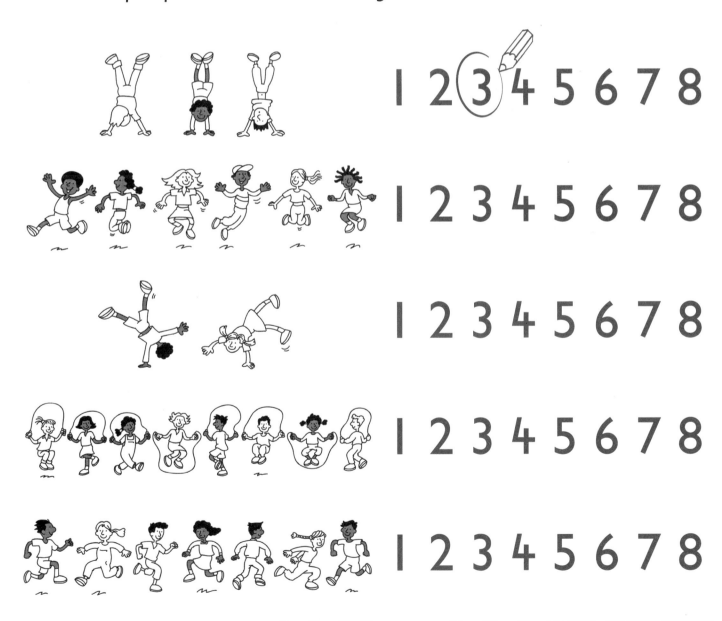

1 2 ③ 4 5 6 7 8

1 2 3 4 5 6 7 8

1 2 3 4 5 6 7 8

1 2 3 4 5 6 7 8

1 2 3 4 5 6 7 8

Number 9

q q q q q q q q q

This girl is counting worms. Draw 9 worms.

Counting to 9

0   1   2   3   4   5   6   7   8   9

Colour 6 socks.

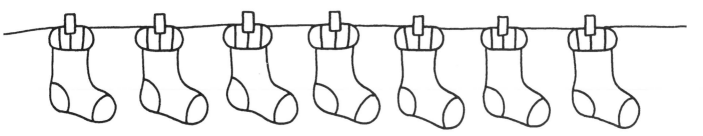

Colour 7 T-shirts.

Colour 8 gloves.

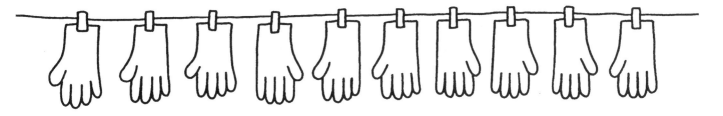

Colour 9 teddies.

Number 10

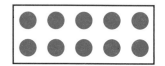

Draw 10 candles. Colour them.

Counting to 10

Count the balloons by joining them to the number line.
Then colour them in.

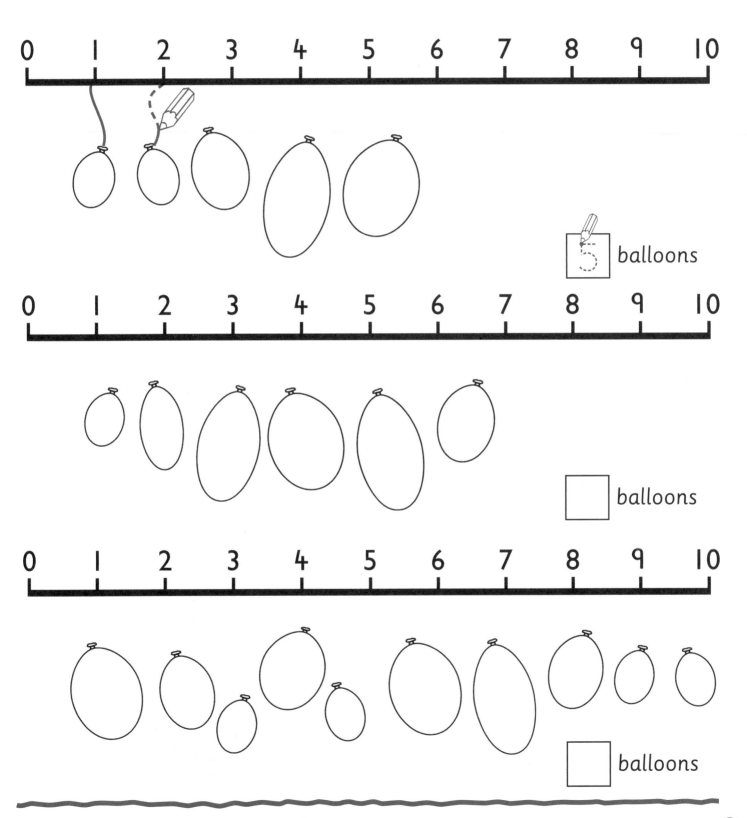

0   1   2   3   4   5   6   7   8   9   10

5 balloons

0   1   2   3   4   5   6   7   8   9   10

☐ balloons

0   1   2   3   4   5   6   7   8   9   10

☐ balloons

Sequencing 0 to 10

Join the dots in number order.

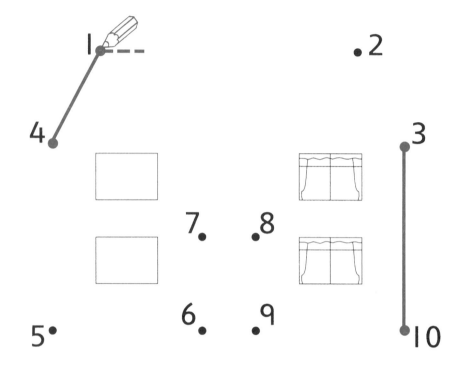

Join the dots in number order.

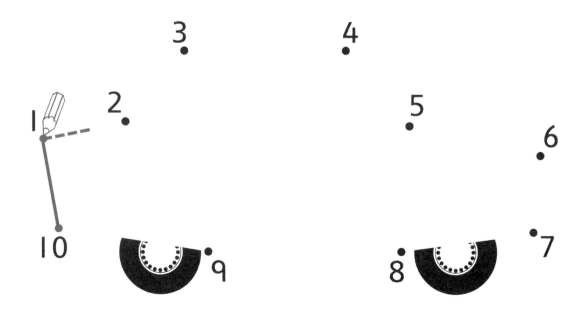

Counting rhyme

Say the rhyme. Point to the numbers as you say them.

1   2   3   4   5
One, two, three, four, five,

Once I caught a fish alive,

6   7   8   9   10
Six, seven, eight, nine, ten,

Then I let it go again.

Join the dots in number order.

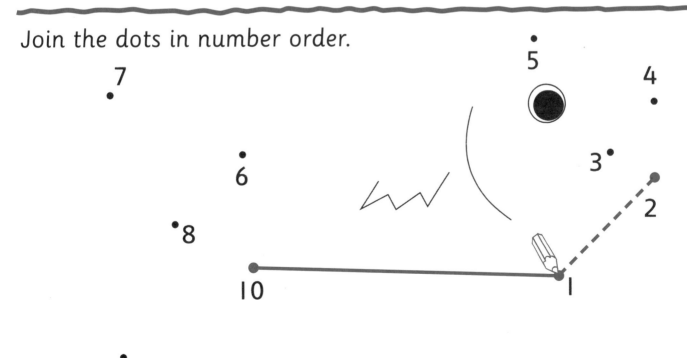

7

5

4

6

3

2

8

10

1

9

Counting

0   1   2   3   4   5   6   7   8   9   10

Number the stones and count how many jumps.

Counting on

0   1   2   3   4   5   6   7   8   9   10

Add one more jump. Write the final number.

Add two more jumps. Write the final number.

Adding sets

0   1   2   3   4   5   6   7   8   9   10

Colour 5 legs green.

Colour 1 leg blue.

Altogether there are ☐ legs.

Colour 8 legs red.

Colour 2 legs yellow.

Altogether there are ☐ legs.

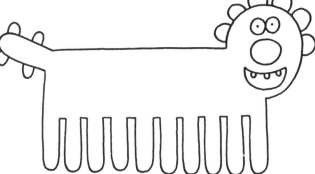

Colour 7 legs orange.

Colour 2 legs brown.

Altogether there are ☐ legs.

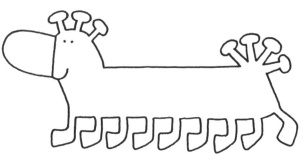

Colour 6 legs pink.

Colour 4 legs black.

Altogether there are ☐ legs.

Number bonds

Colour 9 spots red.

Colour 1 spot blue.

Altogether there are ⬚ spots.

Colour 8 spots green.

Colour 2 spots red.

Altogether there are ⬚ spots.

Colour 7 spots pink.

Colour 3 spots yellow.

Altogether there are ⬚ spots.

Colour 6 spots orange.

Colour 4 spots purple.

Altogether there are ⬚ spots.

Add 1 more

0   1   2   3   4   5   6   7   8   9   10

Add one more biscuit to each plate.

Now there are ☐ biscuits.

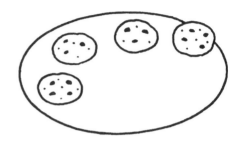

Now there are ☐ biscuits.

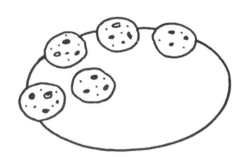

Now there are ☐ biscuits.

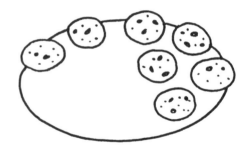

Now there are ☐ biscuits.

Now there are ☐ biscuits.

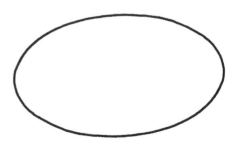

Now there is ☐ biscuit.

More than

Fill in the missing numbers.

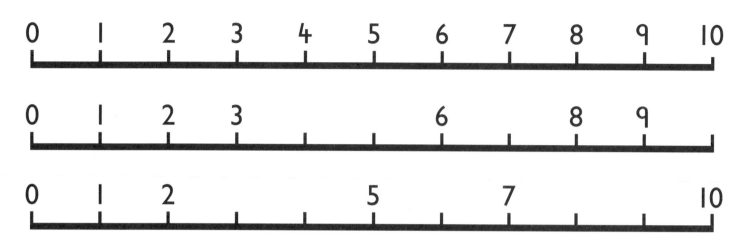

Draw the beads, then write the answer.

One more than 6 is ⬜ 7

One more than 5 is ⬜

One more than 7 is ⬜

One more than 4 is ⬜

Two more than 6 is ⬜

Two more than 5 is ⬜

Two more than 7 is ⬜

Two more than 4 is ⬜

Less than

Fill in the missing numbers.

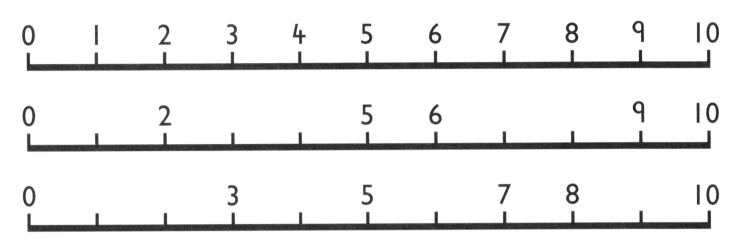

0   1   2   3   4   5   6   7   8   9   10

0   2   5   6   9   10

0   3   5   7   8   10

Draw the beads, then write the answer.

One less than 6 is [5]   ●●●●●✗───────────

One less than 5 is [ ]   ─────────────────

One less than 7 is [ ]   ─────────────────

One less than 4 is [ ]   ─────────────────

Two less than 6 is [ ]   ─────────────────

Two less than 5 is [ ]   ─────────────────

Two less than 7 is [ ]   ─────────────────

Two less than 4 is [ ]   ─────────────────

Take 2 away

0 1 2 3 4 5 6 7 8 9 10

Take 2 pieces of fruit away from each plate.
Count how many are left and fill in the number.

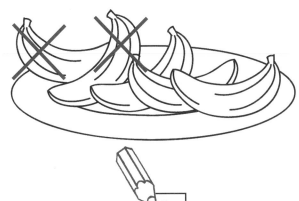

Now there are [3] bananas.

Now there are [ ] apples.

Now there are [ ] cherries.

Now there are [ ] grapes.

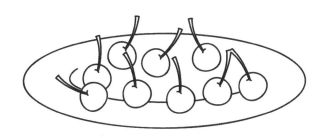

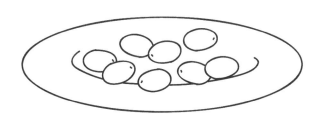

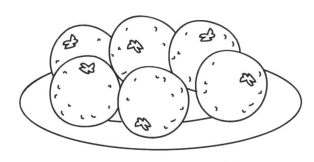

Now there are [ ] oranges.

Now there are [ ] pears.

Numbers 0 to 20

Fill in the missing numbers.

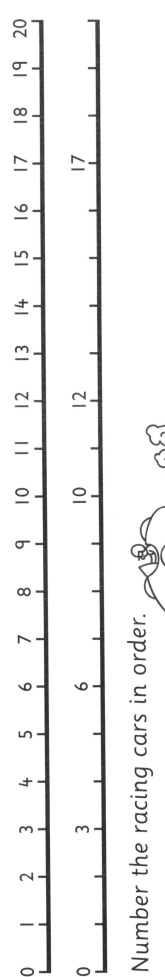

Number the racing cars in order.

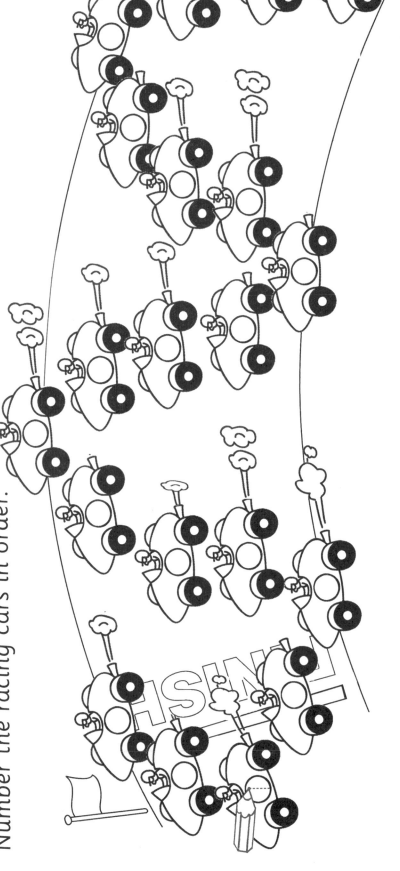

2 at a time

Climb the steps two at a time.
Write the number on top of the step.

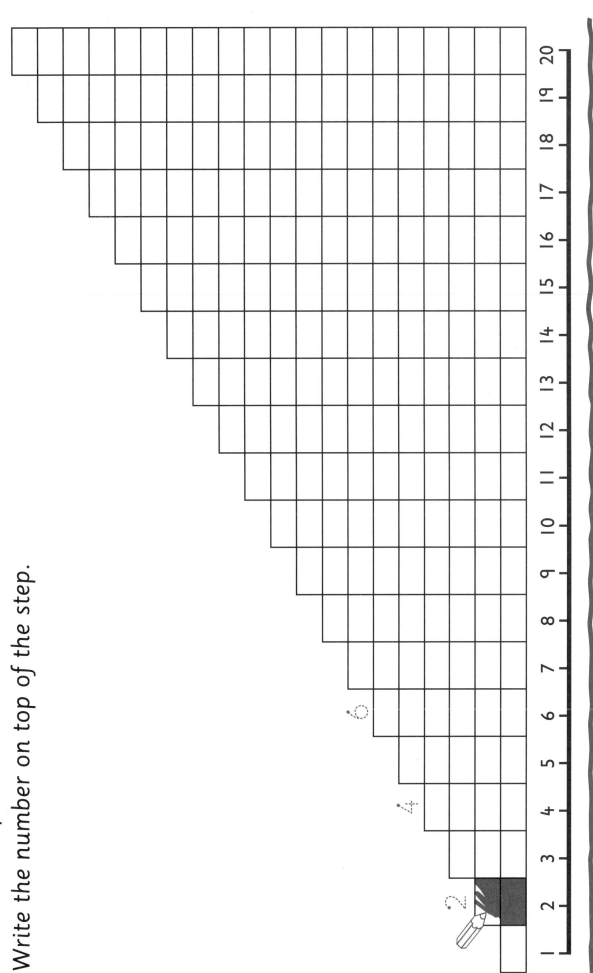

Summary of skills

Fun With Shape and Size

Pack of 6
ISBN-10: 0-19-838433-5

ISBN-13: 978-0-19-838433-5

Pack of 36
ISBN-10: 0-19-838434-3
ISBN-13: 978-0-19-838434-2

Fun With Reading

Pack of 6
ISBN-10: 0-19-838424-6

ISBN-13: 978-0-19-838424-3

Pack of 36
ISBN-10: 0-19-838425-4
ISBN-13: 978-0-19-838425-0

Fun With Writing

Pack of 6
ISBN-10: 0-19-838427-0

ISBN-13: 978-0-19-838427-4

Pack of 36
ISBN-10: 0-19-838428-9
ISBN-13: 978-0-19-838428-1

Fun With Numbers

Pack of 6
ISBN-10: 0-19-838436-X

ISBN-13: 978-0-19-838436-6

Pack of 36
ISBN-10: 0-19-838437-8
ISBN-13: 978-0-19-838437-3

Fun With Counting

Pack of 6
ISBN-10: 0-19-838430-0

ISBN-13: 978-0-19-838430-4

Pack of 36
ISBN-10: 0-19-838431-9
ISBN-13: 978-0-19-838431-1